Be Prese
Not
Perfect

Samuel and Roxan Gardner

ISBN: 9798741462362

A SPECIAL GIFT
just for you

PRESENTED TO

FROM

DATE

For the complex procedure of mind-transformation to take place one has to be a patient in God's operating theatre. Being a patient means being present so an open-heart surgery can be performed. To be reprogrammed from worldly conformation to spiritual transformation requires divine intervention – Samuel E Gardner

PREFACE

Is it your heart's desire to have a closer connection with God and be present with him? Do you sometimes fall short of God's expectations? You may have tried, without success, to quit bad habits, change unfulfilling jobs, break free from toxic relationships or keep away from sexual immorality. As a result, we move further away from actually being present with God.

Today, God is inviting you to be near; to be available; to be ready and he will do the rest. As you make your way through the pages of this 30-day journal you will discover God walking beside you. The scripture verses (New Living Translation), reflections, and prayers will help to keep you focused as you embark on this exciting journey towards a closer relationship with the Lord.

Dedication

We would like to dedicate this book to Joanna Daniel a Mentor and an Inspiration to us

Day 1

Philippians 4:6: Don't worry about anything; instead, pray about everything. Tell God what you need, and thank him for all he has done.

Reflection: To worry is a natural part of our psyche. What do you worry about? We worry when we feel distant from a place of safety, security or a needed solution. Worry is a catalyst for anxiety. Since prayer puts us in the presence of God it creates an atmosphere of peace and assures us that everything is under His control. That's why we can emerge from this quiet place with praise and thanksgiving in our hearts.

_____

_____

_____

_____

_____

_____

_____

_____

_____

_____

_____

_____

_____

_____

_____

_____

_____

_____

_____

_____

_____

Prayer: Lord, help me to bring every worrying thought to you; whatever it may be. Help me to acknowledge that you know what is best for me. Thank you for leading me to the place of prayer when anxiety and stress seem to be getting the best of me, Amen.

Day 2

Romans 12:2: Don't copy the behaviour and customs of this world, but let God transform you into a new person by changing the way you think. Then you will learn to know God's will for you, which is good and pleasing and perfect.

Reflection: Do you know what is God's will for your life? If so, how are you living this out in your daily experience? If you are unsure of what God is calling you to do, you are not alone. Many struggles in this area as well. Deciding to allow God to transform your mind will certainly set you on a path to His purpose. Through prayer and fasting His desire for you will be revealed.

_____

_____

_____

_____

_____

_____

_____

_____

_____

_____

_____

_____

_____

_____

_____

_____

_____

_____

_____

_____

_____

_____

_____

_____

_____

_____

_____

_____

_____

_____

_____

_____

_____

_____

_____

_____

Prayer: Lord, help me to show up and be a willing patient as you reprogram my mind to reflect what is your good and perfect will.

Day 3

Hebrews 13:15: Therefore, let us offer through Jesus a continual sacrifice of praise to God, proclaiming our allegiance to his name.

Reflection: What is your favourite way to praise God? Some people find it easier to praise God when things are going well in their lives. what about you? Do you find it easy to praise when you are in a difficult situation? Our praise must be a continual sacrifice, suggesting that praise should come even when we are going through challenging situations.

_____

_____

_____

_____

_____

_____

_____

_____

_____

_____

_____

_____

_____

_____

_____

_____

_____

_____

_____

_____

_____

_____

_____

_____

Prayer: Lord, help me to offer up praises to you when times are good and even when times are bad. No matter what my circumstances are help me to praise you continually.

Isaiah 43: 18-19: But forget all that - it is nothing compared to what I am going to do. 19 For I am about to do something new. See, I have already begun! Do you not see it? I will make a pathway through the wilderness. I will create rivers in the dry wasteland.

Reflection: Why might God be asking you to forget past blessings? Sometimes we get stuck in the rut of yesterday's failures, misfortunes and regrets. We may find it difficult to move forward. We even get hung up on yesterday's blessings and testimonies about what God has done in the past. Is He asking you to pay attention because He is about to do something new?   Are you present to receive it?

_____

_____

_____

_____

_____

_____

_____

_____

_____

_____

_____

_____

_____

_____

_____

_____

_____

_____

_____

_____

_____

_____

_____

_____

_____

Prayer: Lord, help me to let go of the past, even my past blessings, so I can clearly see the plans you have for my future.

Day 5

Jeremiah 29:11: For I know the plans I have for you," says the Lord. "They are plans for good and not for disaster, to give you a future and a hope.

Reflection: What goals do you have for your life? Have you presented yourself to God so He can reveal His plans for you? We sometimes get caught up with our future endeavours and forget that God wants us to include Him in our life's goals. If you have not already done so how can God be included as part of your plans?

_____

_____

_____

_____

_____

_____

_____

_____

_____

_____

_____

_____

_____

_____

_____

_____

_____

_____

_____

_____

_____

_____

_____

_____

_____

_____

_____

_____

_____

_____

_____

_____

_____

_____

_____

_____

_____

_____

_____

Prayer: Lord, I surrender my plans to you. The plans I have for myself are finite but your plans for me are eternal.

2 Corinthians 5:17: This means that anyone who belongs to Christ has become a new person. The old life is gone; a new life has begun!

Reflection: Belonging to God offers us the privilege of being in His presence. In His presence, we experience newness of life. Renewal requires being present. We dispense with the old and embrace the new. What are some of the things that you are doing that keep you present with God and available for renewal?

_____

_____

_____

_____

_____

_____

_____

_____

_____

_____

_____

_____

_____

_____

_____

_____

_____

_____

_____

_____

_____

Prayer: Lord, I am available to you to be made into a new vessel for your purpose.

Day 7

James 4:14: How do you know what our life will be like tomorrow? Your life is like the morning fog – it's here a little while, then it's gone.

Reflection: Have you considered how fleeting life is - being here this minute and gone the next? Since life is like a fog you should capitalize on every opportunity to be present and available to God. You need not worry about tomorrow. Live to the full in the here and now.

_____

_____

_____

_____

_____

_____

_____

_____

_____

_____

_____

_____

_____

_____

_____

_____

_____

_____

_____

_____

_____

_____

Prayer: Lord, I don't know what my tomorrow will look like but I know who holds tomorrow and I am trusting you to guide me.

Day 8

Philippians 3:16: But we must hold on to the progress we have already made.

Reflection: What progress, if any, are you making to be present and near to God? Sometimes it takes many small steps before we can see any significant change in different areas of our lives. Are there things you will need to drop or get rid of that may be hindering your progress?

_____

_____

_____

_____

_____

_____

_____

_____

_____

_____

_____

_____

_____

_____

_____

_____

_____

_____

_____

_____

_____

_____

_____

_____

_____

_____

_____

_____

_____

_____

_____

_____

_____

_____

_____

_____

Prayer: Lord, I give myself to you. Only you can move me from any circumstance that gets in the way of my progression to know you better and to build a stronger bond with you.

Day 9

Psalms 16:11: You will show me the way of life, granting me the joy of your presence and the pleasures of living with you forever.

Reflection: Have you been able to see the way of life God is trying to show you? What we discover in his presence can be so amazing that it brings joy and pleasure. Seeing what God is showing us helps to clarify our life's purpose.

_____

_____

_____

_____

_____

_____

_____

_____

_____

_____

_____

_____

_____

_____

_____

_____

_____

_____

_____

_____

_____

_____

_____

_____

_____

_____

_____

_____

_____

_____

_____

_____

_____

_____

_____

_____

_____

_____

_____

Prayer: Lord, thank you that I can find joy in your presence. Open my eyes so I can see the way of life you are showing to me.

Day 10

John 3:16: For this is how God loved the world: He gave his one and only Son, so that everyone who believes in him will not perish but have eternal life.

Reflection: Can you fully comprehend the unconditional love God has for us? His love is limitless in its reach. Understanding that God has given heaven's most precious gift to demonstrate His love, being present and available to Him is not too great a sacrifice to make.

_____

_____

_____

_____

_____

_____

_____

_____

_____

_____

_____

_____

_____

_____

_____

_____

_____

_____

_____

_____

_____

_____

_____

_____

_____

_____

_____

Prayer: Lord, please forgive me of any sins I have committed and help me to forgive those who have wronged me. I thank you for your unconditional love for me.

Day 11

Luke 1:37: For the word of God will never fail.

Reflection: Sometimes we try many things but they don't always come out as planned. What have you tried but did not succeed? Do you feel like a failure? Just because you may fail at a particular task, it does not mean that you are a failure. It means that you should either try again until you get it right or try something else.

_____

_____

_____

_____

_____

_____

_____

_____

_____

_____

_____

_____

_____

_____

_____

_____

_____

_____

_____

_____

_____

_____

_____

_____

Prayer: Lord, your word is truth and will never fail. Thank you for being dependable. Help me to trust your word and live up to your expectations.

Day 12

Philippians 4:11: Not that I was ever in need, for I have learned how to be content with whatever I have.

Reflection: Have you been able to try Paul's formula for wealth - it is godliness with contentment. It is for him great gain. That's why he can be content with whatever physical possessions he has. Whether it is a little or a lot he is satisfied. Are you living a life of satisfaction? Do you have contentment with God and what He has seen fit to provide?

_____

_____

_____

_____

_____

_____

_____

_____

_____

_____

_____

_____

_____

_____

_____

_____

_____

_____

_____

_____

_____

_____

_____

_____

_____

_____

_____

_____

_____

_____

_____

_____

_____

_____

_____

_____

_____

Prayer: Lord, I thank you for all the things you have blessed me with. I thank you for life and the people you have put in my path to help make me a better person. Help me to be content with what you have given to me. Most of all thank you for your love.

Day 13

Romans 8:28: And we know that God causes everything to work together for the good of those who love God and are called according to his purpose for them.

Reflection: When we are in a difficult situation, we oftentimes wonder why God seems absent. Then after some time has passed, we realized that God was in the midst all along…has this ever happen to you? Can you recount a particular example when you were going through a difficult period and doubted God's love and care? What have you learnt that has given you the confidence to have a stronger faith in God?

_____

_____

_____

_____

_____

_____

_____

_____

_____

_____

_____

_____

_____

_____

_____

_____

_____

_____

_____

_____

_____

_____

_____

_____

_____

_____

Prayer: Lord, I know you have my best interest at heart and you are working everything out for my good. Help me to put my confidence in you always.

Day 14

Isaiah 41:10: Don't be afraid, for I am with you. Don't be discouraged, for I am your God. I will strengthen you and help you. I will hold you up with my victorious right hand.

Reflection: Is it difficult to be present with God when everything around you is unsettled? The application of the counsel not to be afraid or discouraged only makes sense when we know the ability of the one speaking. Being present with God calms our fears and worries and strengthens us to conquer our mountains.

_____

_____

_____

_____

_____

_____

_____

_____

_____

_____

_____

_____

_____

_____

_____

_____

_____

_____

_____

_____

_____

_____

_____

_____

_____

Prayer: Lord, when I get discourage help me to look to you for strength. I know you will hold me up with your victorious right hand.

Day 15

Revelation 21:4: He will wipe every tear from their eyes, and there will be no more death or sorry or crying or pain. All these things are gone forever."

Reflection: It is often said that tears are a language God understands. But we sometimes hide our tears because we feel other people might think that we are weak. It is always safe to cry in God's presence and unburden before his throne of mercy. We cry now with the certain hope that our tear will be wiped away on that glorious day of His soon return. God knows that some situations will bring tears to our eyes. What has been your experience? How did you deal with the emotion of sadness? How does the future hope of having your tears wiped away help you to cope with your present sorrows?

_____

_____

_____

_____

_____

_____

_____

_____

_____

_____

_____

_____

_____

_____

_____

_____

_____

_____

_____

_____

_____

_____

_____

Prayer: Lord, I look forward to the day when there will be no more sadness and all crying will be over.

Day 16

Psalms 39:7: And so, Lord where do I put my hope? My only hope is in you.

Reflection: The word 'hope' has only four letters but it has endless possibilities. Hope can change a person's life. Have you placed your hope in others who have let you down? What are you hoping for today? Be present with God long enough and you will begin to see your hopes realized.

_____

_____

_____

_____

_____

_____

_____

_____

_____

_____

_____

_____

_____

_____

_____

_____

_____

_____

_____

_____

_____

_____

_____

_____

_____

_____

_____

_____

Prayer: Lord, I put my hope in you.

Day 17

Colossians 4:5 Live wisely among those who are not believers, and make the most of every opportunity.

Reflection: Sharing your faith with non-believers can be daunting at times. It requires being in tune with God every moment. It is important to show our love for God by the way we live as this may be the only way to tell people about God's love. Do you sometimes get opportunities to talk about God to an unbeliever? How have you made the most out of these opportunities?

_____

_____

_____

_____

_____

_____

_____

_____

_____

_____

_____

_____

_____

_____

_____

_____

_____

_____

_____

_____

_____

_____

_____

_____

_____

_____

Prayer: Lord, help me to take advantage of every opportunity to speak to someone about you. Give me wisdom to choose the right words to say.

Day 18

Colossians 4:6: Let your conversation be gracious and attractive so that you will have the right response for everyone.

Reflection: Words can be destructive as well as instructive. The words we use in our conversations can help or worsen a situation. Choosing words wisely requires careful thought. What words are you speaking to yourself and others? Are they helpful or hurtful?

_____

_____

_____

_____

_____

_____

_____

_____

_____

_____

_____

Prayer: Lord put words on my lips that will edify and build. Filter from my mind, words that will cause hurt or pain. Give me wisdom to choose my words well.

Day 19

Isaiah 6:8: Then I heard the Lord asking, "Whom should I send as a messenger to this people? Who will go for us?" I said, "Here I am. Send me."

Reflection: Listening is an important skill but sometimes when we talk to God we don't wait for a response. Can you distinguish the voice of the Lord from among the many voices trying to get your attention? What is God calling you to do? What has been your response?

_____

_____

_____

_____

_____

_____

_____

_____

_____

_____

_____

_____

_____

_____

_____

_____

_____

_____

_____

_____

_____

_____

_____

_____

Prayer: Lord, like Isaiah, give me the willingness not only to listen but to respond to your call.

Day 20

Jeremiah 31:3: Long ago the Lord said to Israel: "I have loved you, my people, with an everlasting love. With unfailing love have I drawn you to myself.

Reflection: God's everlasting love is like a magnet; it keeps drawing His people to Him. Whatever their imperfections He desires them to be close. Do you feel the tug of God's love? God is excited for you to be in His presence.

_____

_____

_____

_____

_____

_____

_____

_____

_____

_____

_____

_____

_____

_____

_____

_____

_____

_____

_____

_____

_____

_____

_____

_____

_____

_____

Prayer: Lord, thank you for loving me with an everlasting love. A love that looks beyond my imperfections to see what my needs truly are.

Day 21

1 Samuel 16:7: But the Lord said to Samuel "Don't judge by his appearance or height, for I have rejected him. The Lord doesn't see things the way you see them. People judge by outward appearance, but the Lord looks at the heart.

Reflection: Like Samuel, we judge things from outward appearances and make assumptions about those we come in contact with. We are also judged by others from our outward appearance; our height, our dress, our looks, even our actions. We sometimes wear masks to disguise our true self. It is both comforting and sobering when we realize that God knows who we are from the inside out. It is comforting because He is confidential and sobering because He would not hide the truth. Is there something hidden to others in your life that you would prefer to even keep hidden from God?

_____

_____

_____

_____

_____

_____

_____

_____

_____

Prayer: Lord, I believe that nothing is hidden from your eyes. I confess my sins to you today. I want to have an authentic, honest and open relationship with you.

Genesis 3:13: I have placed my rainbow in the clouds. It is the sign of my covenant with you and with all the earth.

Reflection: We can take God at His word. He will do what he says. Did you ever receive a promise from someone only for them to go back on their word? What happened and how did you deal with the situation? What promise(s) are you claiming from God today?

_____

_____

_____

_____

_____

_____

_____

_____

_____

_____

_____

_____

_____

_____

_____

_____

_____

_____

_____

_____

_____

_____

_____

_____

Prayer: God, you showed Noah a rainbow as a sign that you will not destroy the world again by a flood. God, your promises are true. I claim them today.

Day 23

Psalms 27:14: Wait for the Lord. Be brave and courageous. Yes, wait patiently for the Lord.

Reflection: The waiting game is one of the hardest to play. It often leads to anxiety. Waiting patiently on God to respond in answer to prayer or for a breakthrough requires being brave and courageous against all the temptations to do things ourselves and in our own way. Have you ever had to wait for anything? How were you able to handle the temptations to do your own thing?

_____

_____

_____

_____

_____

_____

_____

_____

_____

_____

_____

Prayer: Lord, waiting can be difficult but give me the patience to wait when I need to.

Day 24

Philippians 2:3: Don't be selfish; don't try to impress others. Be humble, thinking of others as better than yourselves.

Reflection: Paul's appeal warns us against projecting ourselves to impress others. When we care genuinely about others, we tend to look for the good in them. Humility allows us to treat them even better than ourselves. What does humility mean to you as you relate to others?

_____

_____

_____

_____

_____

_____

_____

_____

_____

_____

_____

_____

_____

_____

_____

_____

_____

_____

_____

_____

_____

_____

_____

_____

Prayer: Lord, help me to show love to others in a way that is not boastful or proud. Help me to love others as you love, without selfishness.

Day 25

Galatians 4:7: Now you are no longer a slave but God's own child. And since you are his child, God has made you his heir.

Reflection: In Christ we are free. Sin cannot keep us captive. Are you being held back by something that is causing you to drift away from God? Something that seems to be holding you captive? What are you doing today to break free?

_____

_____

_____

_____

_____

_____

_____

_____

_____

_____

_____

_____

_____

_____

_____

_____

_____

_____

_____

_____

_____

_____

_____

Prayer: Lord, I am weak but you are strong. I need your help to rescue me from the stronghold of the enemy. Thanks for reminding me that I can be free and no longer a slave to sin.

Day 26

Psalms 139:14: Thank you for making me so wonderfully complex! Your workmanship is marvelous – how well I know it.

Reflection: The human body is a biological and engineering marvel. We are indeed fearfully and wonderfully made. Made in the image of God, we have been created for a high and holy purpose. Whatever we achieve through the use of our body and mind is a testament to the amazing workmanship of our creator. What have you been able to achieve with the use of your body and mind? How has spending time in God's presence honed these gifts for His service?

_____

_____

_____

_____

_____

_____

_____

_____

_____

_____

_____

_____

_____

_____

_____

_____

_____

_____

_____

_____

_____

_____

_____

Prayer: Lord and Creator, help me to appreciate how wonderful I am as a product of your hand. Use my mind and body; let them bring honour and glory to you.

Day 27

Psalms 27:1: The Lord is my light and my salvation – so why should I be afraid? The Lord is my fortress, protecting me from danger, so why should I tremble?

Reflection: Fear is a natural emotion. It can keep us safe but it can also cripple us if we allow it to take over our lives. What makes you afraid? Allowing the Lord to be your salvation and fortress protects you from those things or situations that induce fear.

_____

_____

_____

_____

_____

_____

_____

_____

_____

_____

_____

_____

_____

_____

_____

_____

_____

_____

_____

_____

_____

_____

_____

_____

Prayer: Lord, help me to overcome the fear that clouds my eyes from seeing you as my light, salvation and fortress.

Day 28

Isaiah 22:22: I will give him the key to the house of David – the highest position in the royal court. When he opens doors, no one will be able to close them; when he closes them; no one will be able to open them.

Reflection: When God wants to elevate you there is nothing that can stop it from happening; not even events that took place in your past. Are you in the position for God to elevate you? Are you available to him?

_____

_____

_____

_____

_____

_____

_____

_____

_____

_____

_____

_____

_____

_____

_____

_____

_____

_____

_____

_____

_____

_____

_____

_____

_____

_____

_____

_____

_____

_____

_____

_____

_____

_____

Prayer: Lord, I know that you can make me the head and not the tail. You have cast my sins away and remembered them no more. Help me to move into the position you have ordained for me knowing that you alone are the key holder.

Day 29

1 Peter 3:15: Instead, you must worship Christ as Lord of your life. And if someone asks about your hope as a believer, always be ready to explain it.

Reflection: A natural outgrowth of worship is confession. Having truly worshipped we are led to share our experience of the hope we have in Christ. Are you ready to give an answer for the hope you have in Christ?

_____

_____

_____

_____

_____

_____

_____

_____

_____

_____

_____

_____

_____

Be Present Not Perfect

_____

_____

_____

_____

_____

_____

_____

_____

_____

_____

_____

_____

Prayer: Lord, let my worship experience with you prepare me to share the hope I have in you with others.

Day 30

Psalms 139:17: How precious are your thoughts about me, O God. They cannot be numbered!

Reflection: We get excited when someone we care about tells us that they are thinking about us. God thoughts towards us are numberless and precious. Knowing that we are on God's mind gives us a sense of our value and worth to Him. How has knowing that you are on God's mind motivated you?

_____

_____

_____

_____

_____

_____

_____

_____

_____

_____

_____

_____

_____

_____

_____

_____

_____

_____

_____

_____

_____

_____

_____

_____

_____

_____

_____

_____

_____

_____

_____

_____

_____

_____

_____

Prayer: Lord, knowing that you have precious thoughts about me reminds me of how valuable I am to you. Help me to always remember this when I am facing difficult times. Help me to stay in your presence always, AMEN!

Printed in Great Britain
by Amazon